**DEPARTMENT OF THE NAVY**
HEADQUARTERS UNITED STATES MARINE CORPS
WASHINGTON, DC 20380-0001

I0500623

# PRODUCT QUALITY DEFICIENCY REPORT (PQDR)

**DEPARTMENT OF THE NAVY**
HEADQUARTERS UNITED STATES MARINE CORPS
WASHINGTON, DC 20380-0001

MCO 4855.10B
LPP
26 Jan 93

MARINE CORPS ORDER 4855.10B

From: Commandant of the Marine Corps
To:   Distribution List

Subj: PRODUCT QUALITY DEFICIENCY REPORT (PQDR)

Ref:  (a) SECNAVINST 4855.5 (NOTAL)
      (b) MIL-STD-109B (NOTAL)
      (c) MCO 4105.2
      (d) MCO P4130.8
      (e) DoDDir 4000.25 (NOTAL)
      (f) DoDDir 4155.1 (NOTAL)
      (g) SECNAVINST P5212.5C (NOTAL)
      (h) MCO 5210.11D

Encl: (1) Definitions
      (2) Exemptions
      (3) Sample Message Format for the Category I Product
          Quality Deficiency Report
      (4) Sample Electronic Mail (E-Mail) for the Category I
          Product Quality Deficiency Report
      (5) Sample Product Quality Deficiency Report
      (6) Instructions for Preparation of the Product Quality
          Deficiency Report (SF 368)
      (7) Originating Point Procedures
      (8) Screening Point Procedures
      (9) Action Point Procedures
      (10) PQDR Exhibit Procedures
      (11) Output Requirements for Marine Corps Quality
           Deficiency Information System

Report Required:  Product Quality Deficiency Report (Report
                  Control Symbol EXEMPT), par. 7

1. <u>Purpose</u>.  To prescribe policy and procedures for Marine Corps
units and to assign specific responsibilities facilitating
submission and processing of PQDR's, Standard Form (SF) 368, as
defined in reference (a).  External agencies assigned action on
PQDR's will be guided by reference (a).

2. <u>Cancellation</u>.  MCO 4855.10A.

3. <u>Summary of Revision</u>.  Extensive changes have been made to
this Order and it should be reviewed in its entirety.  The format
used herein provides a comprehensive breakdown of the procedures
and responsibilities, and delineates the functions as they relate
to standard reporting and processing criteria.  Many other system
improvements have been incorporated.

4. <u>Definitions</u>. Definitions of terms associated with PQDR processing are contained in enclosure (1). Additional definitions are contained in reference (b).

5. <u>Objective</u>. The primary goals of the program are to maximize mission and operational effectiveness, prevent recurring deficiencies, and improve user satisfaction with Marine Corps materiel.

    a. Provide a user product quality deficiency reporting and a data feedback system that provides for appropriate documentation, action/resolution, and specific points of contact (POC) for all phases of PQDR processing.

    b. Provide for analysis and investigation of PQDR's in a timely manner for expedient corrective and preventive actions.

    c. Provide for control and disposition of deficient materiel.

    d. Maintain a system that affords management with visibility of PQDR summary data, identification of problems, recurring deficiencies, and resolution/corrective actions.

6. <u>Policy</u>. Equipment having deficiencies that meet the reporting criteria for a PQDR will be reported and processed using the procedures outlined in this Order. Additionally, investigation into and resolution of these reported deficiencies will be expedient and field activities will be notified of the corrective actions.

7. <u>Action</u>. Qualifications and procedures for the processing of PQDR's are as follows:

    a. The PQDR process begins with the user/originator reporting the materiel deficiency to the originating point, as depicted in figure 1. The figure outlines the general path of the PQDR and the most crucial actions/decisions that are dependent on prescribed timeframe criteria. Note: The term "Screening Point" is defined as Commander, Marine Corps Logistics Bases (Code 808), Albany, Georgia.

    b. A PQDR shall be submitted as a result of any of the circumstances listed below:

       (1) A physical or operational condition considered to constitute a hazard to personnel or materiel.

       (2) A design of items or components which impedes the proper operation, maintenance, or handling of the materiel or item.

       (3) Faulty materiel or poor workmanship.

<u>User/Originator</u>      - Prepare PQDR

                    - Determine the level of severity

                       -- Compare with severity categories

                    - Forward report to the originating point

<u>Originating Point</u>    - Check for validity, completeness, and accuracy of report

                    - Validate the level of severity

                       -- Assign report control number

                       -- Compare with severity categories

                    - Forward the report to the screening point

<u>Screening Point</u>     - Certify validity, completeness, and accuracy of report

                    - Certify level of severity category

                    - Acknowledge receipt to sender

                       -- Apply timeframe criteria

                    - Advise sender of any nonconcurrence or change of category

                    - Determine appropriate action point

                       -- By contracting agency, action point, type commodity, etc.

                    - Forward PQDR to action point

Figure 1.--Outline of the PQDR Process and Actions.

Action Point          - Acknowledge receipt of PQDR to
                        screening point

                        -- Apply timeframe criteria

                      - Determine cause of deficiency

                      - If invalid, inform screening point

                      - Use support point, if necessary

                        -- Provide technical evaluation when
                           required

                      - Determine if credit applies

Support Point         - Acknowledge receipt to action point

                        -- Apply timeframe criteria

                      - Determine cause of deficiency

                      - Provide technical evaluation when
                        required

                      - If invalid, inform action point

                      - Determine whether credit applies

                      - Respond to action point

Screening Point       - Review recommendation of action point

                      - Respond to originator and all
                        appropriate commands and customers

                      All the above actions should be
                      accomplished within required
                      timeframes.

Figure 1.--Outline of the PQDR Process and Actions--Continued.

(4) Excessive wear or deterioration for the period of time and for the conditions under which the item was in use or on hand.

(5) Operation or performance of equipment in the course of normal operations that fail to meet stated operational limits.

(6) Circumstances other than those indicated herein but considered to be related to deficiencies in materiel quality and not meeting the reporting criteria for other programs listed in enclosure (2).

(7) Tactical systems computer software/firmware and documentation deficiencies. See enclosure (1).

(8) Items known to be under warranty shall be reported on SF 368 per special instructions contained in the materiel fielding plan (MFP) issued per reference (c) or supply instructions (SI).

c. Exemptions to the above criteria are provided in enclosure (2).

d. The reporting and processing of PQDR's will be accomplished in timeframes that are prescribed by level of severity categories. Each valid PQDR will satisfy the criteria for one of two categories; Category I (Cat I), Category II (Cat II). The required timeframes for the handling, processing, and completion of PQDR's are delineated in figure 2.

e. The validity of the PQDR will be established early in the processing stages and will be monitored in all stages of processing through resolution.

f. <u>Reporting Procedures</u>

(1) The user/originator shall report all materiel deficiencies to the originating point (defined in enclosure (1)). The originating point shall check the validity of the PQDR by comparison with the criteria of paragraphs 7b and c, preceding. The originating point shall assign one of the levels of severity categories (Cat I/Cat II) (defined in enclosure (1) under paragraphs 3 and 4).

(2) The originator shall complete the SF 368 per enclosures (3) through (6) and shall provide an original and two copies to the screening point via the originating point. It is essential that the originator report as completely and clearly as possible all available information applicable to the defective materiel.

| Reporting/Processing Component | Severity Category | Action and Timeframe for Response |
|---|---|---|
| (1) Originator | Cat I | Forward report to originating point within 24 hours after discovery |
| | | Submit SF 368 within: |
| | Cat I | 48 hours after forwarding to originating point if supporting documents will aid the investigation |
| | Cat II | 3 days after discovery |
| (2) Originating Point | Cat I | Notify Commander, MARCORLOGBASES, Albany, by message, electronic mail (E-Mail), or electronic facsimile within 24 hours after receipt from originator |
| | | Submit SF 368 within: |
| | Cat 1 | 48 hours after sending message if supporting documents will aid the investigation |
| | Cat II | 3 days after discovery |
| (3) Screening Point | | Acknowledge receipt to originator within: |
| | Cat I | 24 hours after receiving message |
| | Cat II | 10 days after receiving SF 368 |
| | | Forward to action point within: |
| | Cat I | 24 hours after receiving message |
| | Cat II | 10 days after receiving SF 368 |
| | | Final response to originator within: |
| | Cat I | 3 days after receiving response from action point |
| | Cat II | 3 days after receiving response from action point |

Figure 2.--PQDR Response Matrix.

| Reporting/Processing Component | Severity Category | Action and Timeframe for Response |
|---|---|---|
| (4)  Action Point | | Acknowledge receipt to screening point within: |
| | Cat I | 24 hours after receiving PQDR for action |
| | Cat II | 10 days after receiving SF 368 |
| | | Suspend/screen stock within: |
| | Cat I | 24 hours after receiving PQDR or electronic facsimile |
| | Cat II | 20 days after receiving SF 368 |
| | | Forward to support point when assistance is required within: |
| | Cat I | 24 hours after receiving message, E-Mail, or electronic facsimile |
| | Cat II | 10 days after receiving SF 368 |
| | | Provide an interim or final reply to screening point within: |
| | Cat I | 20 days w/o exhibit or 20 days after receipt of requested exhibit |
| | Cat II | 30 days w/o exhibit or 30 days after receipt of requested exhibit |
| | | Forward replies from support point to screening point within: |
| | Cat I | 3 days after receiving message, E-Mail, or electronic facsimile |
| | Cat II | 10 days after receiving SF 368 |
| (5)  Support Point | | Acknowledge receipt to action point within: |
| | Cat I | 24 hours after receiving message, E-Mail, or electronic facsimile |

Figure 2.--PQDR Response Matrix--Continued.

7

| Reporting/Processing Component | Severity Category | Action and Timeframe for Response |
|---|---|---|
| | Cat II | 10 days after receiving SF 368 |
| | | _Provide an interim or final reply to action point within:_ |
| | Cat I | 20 days w/o exhibit or 20 days after receipt of requested exhibit |
| | Cat II | 30 days w/o exhibit or 30 days after receipt of requested exhibit |

Figure 2.--PQDR Response Matrix--Continued.

(a) The originating point shall submit separate PQDR's for each deficiency identified which meets the criteria of paragraph 7b, preceding.  Identical deficiencies of the same item may be consolidated in one report.  In those cases where one deficiency is either the cause or the result of another deficiency, the originating point shall report each deficiency separately and shall reference the other in each respective report for the purpose of facilitating trend analysis by the screening point or action point.

(b) The originating point shall furnish, as enclosures to the PQDR, any photographs, negatives, drawings, sketches, and/or illustrations of the defective item, if easily transportable/ mailable.

(c) The unit/activity which submits the report shall retain the defective part(s)/sample(s) as an exhibit, pending receipt of disposition instructions from the screening point. Figure (3) depicts the process matrix for the disposition/shipping of exhibits.

(3) The originating point shall follow the procedures provided in enclosure (7).  These procedures outline critical timeframes that vary per the severity category cited in paragraph 7f(1), preceding.

(4) As an alternate method to the previous paragraph, the originator may produce a facsimile of the SF 368 by electronic means.  The facsimile must duplicate the format of the SF 368 as revised October 1985, or as subsequently revised.  However, the completed SF 368 facsimile must continue to be mailed to the Marine Corps Screening Point until such time as the screening point obtains the capability to receive PQDR's via electronic transmission.

g.  Screening point and action point procedures are contained in enclosures (8) and (9), respectively.

h.  Exhibit procedures are contained in enclosure (10). Failure to meet the specified timeframes may result in the PQDR being closed without complete investigation.

8.  Responsibilities

a.  Commander, MARCORLOGBASES, Albany, GA, shall:

(1) Establish policy for the Marine Corps PQDR Program.

(2) Review monthly the Management Summary Data of Marine Corps Quality Deficiency Information Systems (MCQDIS).

(3) Serve as the central POC for the Marine Corps PQDR Program.

MCO 4855.10B
26 Jan 93

| ORIGINATOR ORIGINATING POINT | SCREENING POINT | ACTION POINT | SUPPORT POINT |
|---|---|---|---|
| Tag exhibit with DD Form 1575 and DD Form 2332. | When exhibit is requested by action point conducting independent investigation, provide shipping instructions to originating point (Cat I - 5 days max; Cat II - 10 days max). | When action point conducts independent investigation and exhibit is required, request exhibit within 15 days after receipt of PQDR from screening point or, if authorized, directly from originating (holding) point. | |
| Hold exhibit until disposition instructions received. Follow up to appropriate screening or action point after 60 days. | Provide exhibit disposition instructions to originating point if PQDR is terminated or exhibit is unnecessary (10 days max). | | |
| | Provide exhibit disposition instructions to originating point if action point terminates PQDR or determines exhibit is unnecessary. | Provide exhibit disposition instructions to screening point if PQDR is terminated or unnecessary (10 days max). | Request exhibit from action point or if authorized directly from originating (holding) point within 7 days after receipt of PQDR if required for the investigation. |
| After receipt of shipping authority, ship exhibit to action or support point. A copy of shipping document shall be furnished the screening point on all exhibit movement. Category I exhibits within 3 days. Category II exhibits within 6 days. Notify screening point of shipment. | When exhibit is requested by support point and the shipping instructions are forwarded by action point, provide instructions to originating point (3 days max). | When exhibit is requested by support point, provide shipping instructions to screening point (Cat I - 5 days max; Cat II - 10 days max) and concurrently provide disposition instructions to support point for the exhibit after completion of the investigation. | Notify action point within 10 days of exhibit receipt and exhibit disposition. |
| | | | Initiate action to dispose of exhibit after final investigation reply is sent to action point per enclosure (10). |

NOTE: All times are calendar days.

Figure 3.--Disposition and Shipping Instructions of Exhibits.

10

PRODUCT QUALITY DEFICIENCY REPORT EXHIBIT

| 1. REPORT CONTROL NUMBER | 2. DATE (YYMMDD) | 3. ORIGINATING ACTIVITY |
| 4. NSN | 5. PART NO. | 6. SERIAL NO. |
| 7. REMARKS (Continue on reverse, if necessary) | 8. ITEM DESCRIPTION | |
| | 9. NAME (Last, First, Middle Initial) | 10. PHONE (Include Area Code) |

DD Form 2332, JUL 88          Previous edition is obsolete.          S/N 0102-LF-D07-3740          59/188

| FSN, PART NO. AND ITEM DESCRIPTION | | SUSPENDED TAG-MATERIEL | |
| | | NEXT INSPECTION DUE | CONDITION CODE |
| | | INSPECTION ACTIVITY | |
| | | REASON OR AUTHORITY | |
| SERIAL NUMBER/LOT NO. | UNIT OF ISSUE | | |
| CONTRACT OR PURCHASE ORDER NO. | QUANTITY | INSPECTOR'S NAME OR STAMP AND DATE | |
| REMARKS | | | |

★ U.S. GPO 1990-707-184

WARNING: Unauthorized persons removing, defacing, or destroying this tag may be subject to a fine of not more than $1,000 or imprisonment for not more than one year or both.     (18 USC 1361)

DD FORM 1575   1 OCT. 66   S/N 0102-LF-016-0400

Figure 4.-- DD Forms 2332 and 1575.

11

(4) Maintain the central data collection point for providing the input to the MCQDIS. Maintain the output of the MCQDIS as described in enclosure (11).

(5) Prepare analysis of the PQDR's as requested in enclosure (8).

(6) Maintain a central screening point for all Marine Corps PQDR's per reference (a).

(7) Initiate PQDR's per paragraph 7f, preceding, when applicable.

(8) Publish applicable Modification Instruction (MI)/Technical Instruction (TI) resulting from approved Engineering Change Proposals (ECP).

b. <u>Commander, Marine Corps Systems Command (COMMARCORSYSCOM) (PSE) shall</u>:

(1) Review and evaluate trend analyses received from Commander, MARCORLOGBASES, Albany, and provide recommended action(s) to the appropriate COMMARCORSYSCOM Branch.

(2) Review appropriate ECP's resulting from corrective action per references (d) and (e).

(3) Coordinate all COMMARCORSYSCOM requests for quality deficiency trend analyses.

(4) Provide support to COMMARCORSYSCOM action points upon their request. COMMARCORSYSCOM action points will process PQDR's per enclosure (9).

(5) Maintain a system or systems that feedback information per reference (f) to correct/prevent quality problems.

c. <u>CO, Marine Corps Tactical System Support Activity (MCTSSA), Camp Pendleton, shall</u>:

(1) Process tactical systems computer firmware, software, and documentation deficiencies, per the action point procedures of enclosure (9).

(2) Initiate PQDR's per paragraph 7f, when applicable.

(3) Draft applicable MI's/TI's resulting from approved ECP's, and forward to Commander, MARCORLOGBASES, Albany, for publication.

9. <u>Activities Submitting PQDR's.</u> All activities shall comply with the provisions of this Order.

10.  Availability of Forms.  SF 368, National Stock Number (NSN)
7540-00-133-5541; DD Form 2332, NSN 0102-LF-007-6400; and DD Form
1575, NSN 0102-LF-016-0400 are available through normal supply
procedures.  DD Forms 2332 and 1575 are depicted in figure 4.

11.  Records.  Records are a principal form of objective evidence.
It is, therefore, essential that each activity retain records per
references (g) and (h).  Activities shall retain records
indefinitely for all PQDR's for which they have not received notice
of any closing action from the Marine Corps Screening Point.

12.  Reserve Applicability.  This Order is applicable to the Marine
Corps Reserve.


R.A.TI4
R. A. TIEBOUT
Deputy Chief of Staff
for Installations and Logistics

DISTRIBUTION:     10206610700

    Copy to:     7000160 (25)
                 7000110 (50)
                 7230026 (5)
                 7000093/144 (1)
                 8145001 (1)
                 7256087 (25)

DEFINITIONS

1. Action Point. A focal point(s), identified within each service/agency, command/component, or contractor, which is responsible for resolution of a reported product quality deficiency including necessary collaboration with support points. Only an action point is authorized to transmit a deficiency report to a support point.

2. Action Reports. A deficiency report addressed to an activity or forwarded to an activity with a request for assistance to investigate and resolve the deficiency/discrepancy or to obtain disposition or audit instructions for like defective materiel.

3. Category I Deficiency. A product quality deficiency which may cause death, injury, or severe occupational illness; would cause loss of or major damage to a weapon system; directly restricts the combat readiness capabilities of a using organization; or which would result in a production line stoppage.

4. Category II Deficiency. A product quality deficiency which does not meet the criteria set forth for category I.

5. Closure. PQDR's may be considered closed when an investigation into the assignable cause has been completed; corrective actions to preclude recurrence of the deficiency have been initiated; and credit instructions and disposition instructions for the materiel have been provided. A PQDR may also be considered closed when MARCORLOGBASES (Code 808-1), Albany determines that it is in the best interest of the Government/USMC that the PQDR be considered closed.

6. Computer Program Documentation. Technical data or information, including computer listings and printouts, which document the requirements, design, or details of computer software, explains the capabilities and limitations of the software, or provides operating instructions for using or supporting computer software during the software's operational life.

7. Design Deficiency. Any condition that limits or prevents the use of materiel for the purpose intended or required, where the materiel meets all other specifications or contractual requirements. These deficiencies cannot be corrected except through a design or specification change.

8. Exhibit. The item reported as being deficient, or a sample item which represents the reported deficient condition, which can be analyzed to determine the possible cause of the defect.

9. _Government-Furnished Property_.  Property in the possession of or acquired directly by the Government and subsequently delivered to or otherwise made available to the contractor.

10. _Government-Owned Product_.  A product which is owned by or leased to the Government or acquired by the Government under the terms of a contract.

11. _Information Only Report_.  A deficiency report sent as a "copy furnished" or "information copy" or one whose transmittal letter states that the report is furnished for information.  A written response to the originator is not required.

12. _New Materiel_.  Materiel procured under contract from commercial or Government sources or manufactured by an in-house facility.  Such materiel will be considered new until it has been proven during actual system operation.

13. _Materiel Deficiency_.  An unsatisfactory condition (for example, physical, chemical, software, firmware, electrical, functional) noted in materiel which is attributable to nonconformance to contractual or specification requirements. Substandard workmanship and manufacturing defects will be considered to fall within this definition provided the standard against which the work has been judged is identified.

14. _Marine Corps Quality Deficiency Information System (MCQDIS)_. An automated system that provides for accountability, trend analysis, and detailed management of deficiency information reported on equipment.

15. _Objective Evidence_.  Documentation which supports a determination that a deficiency exists.  This may include the results of tests, inspections, or other examinations, photographs, video recordings, or other visual recordings, etc.

16. _Originating Point_.  The unit that finds a product quality deficiency and reports it to the screening point.  A unit in this case is defined as a Marine Corps organization operating under an approved table of organization and assigned a reporting unit code (RUC).  (Normally Battalion/Squadron/Separate Company in the FMF. Like equivalent or specific activity in the supporting establishment, e.g. battalion, PX activity, etc.)

17. _Procurement Deficiency_.  Any unsatisfactory materiel condition which is attributable to improper, incorrect, ambiguous, omitted, or conflicting contractual requirements including the procurement document it references, or any combination which describes technical requirements of materiel.

18. _Product_.  Item, materiel, software, supplies, system, assembly, subassembly, or portion thereof which is produced, purchased, developed, or otherwise used by the Government.

19. <u>Product Quality Deficiency</u>. A defect or nonconforming condition which limits or prohibits the item from fulfilling its intended purpose. Included are deficiencies in design, specifications, materiel, manufacturing, operation, and workmanship.

20. <u>Product Quality Deficiency Report (PQDR)</u>. The SF 368 form or other approved format used to record and transmit product quality deficiency data.

21. <u>Quality Deficiency Data</u>. Information (based on objective evidence) provided by an activity concerning unsatisfactory (government or contractor) materiel. The data can be as simple as the originating point's internal report form that initially recorded the deficiency. Of prime importance is the requirement for documentation which is based on direct examination, test, procedural review, etc.

22. <u>Quality Investigation</u>. A comprehensive investigation conducted by the action and support points to determine whether the reported unsatisfactory materiel was repaired, manufactured, or tested in conformance to required specifications, standards, or contractual requirements and that applicable quality controls are adequate to ensure conformance.

23. <u>Reworked Materiel</u>. Materiel which has been overhauled, rebuilt, repaired, reworked, or modified by a military facility or commercial facility and proven during actual system operation.

24. <u>Screening Point</u>. The Marine Corps central point responsible for processing the input and output to the MCQDIS (Commander (Code 808-1), MARCORLOGBASES, Albany, GA 31704-5000), whose responsibilities shall be independent and separate from the responsibilities performed by the action point. A focal point that reviews the PQDR for proper categorization, validity, correctness of entries, accuracy, and completion of information addresses; determines and transmits PQDR to the proper action point within or outside the Marine Corps; maintains an audit trail for each PQDR; reviews close-out responses from action points; and collects, maintains, and exchanges PQDR data.

25. <u>Support Point</u>. Any functional area that assists the action point, as requested, by conducting and providing results of a special analysis or investigation pertinent to the correction and prevention of a reported product quality deficiency.

26. <u>Tactical System Software and Support</u>. Computer resources acquired for use as integral parts of weapons, command and control, communications, intelligence, and other tactical or strategic systems aboard ships, aircraft, and shore facilities and their

support systems.  The term also includes all computer resources associated with specific program developmental test and evaluation, operational test and evaluation, and post-deployment software support including weapon system trainer devices, automatic test equipment, land-based test sites, and system integration and test environments.

27.  Test Deficiencies.  Any incompatibility or failure of materiel as measured against the applicable test specifications, procedures, or test equipment between Government or contractor cognizant activities.

28.  User/Originator.  The person who becomes aware of a defect or deficiency and reports it to the originating point.

EXEMPTIONS

1. The following deficiencies are exempt from this Order:

a. Receipt of overages, shortages, missing documentation, wrong item, packing, marking, and similar deficiencies on shipments, and items listed in Stock List 3/Master Component Lists. These shall be reported as a Report of Discrepancy, SF 364, per MCO 4430.3.

b. Foreign Military Sales items under the Security Assistance (SA) Program after conveyance of the title. Quality deficiency data under the SA Program are properly reported on the Report of Discrepancy, SF 364. These shall be reported per MCO 4140.1.

c. Materiel that fails because user-performed maintenance was inadequate or the materiel was operated improperly; or materiel that fails due to normal wear and tear.

d. Class V(W) materiel deficiencies. These shall be reported per MCO 8025.1.

e. Nuclear weapons materiel deficiencies. These shall be reported per Navy SWOP 5-8.

f. Transportation-type discrepancies, e.g.; shortages, losses, or damages intransit, are reported on the Transportation Discrepancy Report, SF 361. These shall be reported per MCO P4610.19.

g. Accidental damage.

h. Deficiencies found during qualification testing of materiel for acceptance by the Marine Corps or other Government agencies, other than receipt/incoming inspections and tests.

i. Erroneous instruction or discrepancies found in the content of technical publications which would jeopardize operation, mainte- nance, or performance of the item or equipment supported shall be reported per MCO P5215.17. (This excludes general typographical errors not affecting operation, maintenance, or performance.)

j. Aeronautical equipment deficiencies. These shall be reported per OPNAVINST 4790.2.

k. Subsistence item complaints. These shall be reported on a DD Form 1608 per MCO's 10110.21 and 10110.38.

l. Medical materiel complaints. These shall be reported on a Medical Materiel Complaint, SF 380, per Defense Logistics Agency Regulations (DLAR) 4155.28.

   m.  Deficiencies involving products authorized for local base
or station purchase which are reportable under local procedures to
the contracting officer.  This exclusion does not apply to local
purchases where the original source was the General Services
Administration (GSA).

   n.  Any unsatisfactory materiel condition which is attributable
to improper handling or deterioration during storage.  Report per
local procedures.

SAMPLE MESSAGE FORMAT FOR THE CATEGORY I
PQDR

1.  General Information

    a.  Category I PQDR's shall be reported electronically by message, E-Mail, or electronic facsimile of the SF 368 as shown in enclosures (3) through (5).  Category I PQDR's shall' be followed up by the SF 368 report as set forth in enclosures (5) through (7) only when supporting documents will aid the investigation. Deficient equipment under warranty shall be reported per the implementing warranty clauses, SI's, or MFP's.

    b.  All items should be completed and particular importance given to inclusion of the purchasing document number and the contract number.  If an entry is not applicable (N/A) to the deficiency being reported, enter "N/A."  The format and illustrations of entries are shown in enclosures (3) through (5). Messages are keyed to the applicable entries on the SF 368 (enclosure (5)).  The detailed instructions for each item entry are described in enclosure (6).

UNCLASSIFIED

01   03                    PP        UUUU                          2301430

   ADMIN

                  ORIGINATING POINT//MMO//

                  COMMARCORLOGBASES ALBANY GA//808-1//

               INFO AIG ONE ONE TWO ONE SIX//MMO//

UNCLAS //N04855//

SUBJ:   PRODUCT QUALITY DEFICIENCY REPORT

MSGID/GENADMIN/COMMARCORLOGBASESALB/ 808-1//

RMKS/1.   THE FOLLOWING SF 368 BLOCKS APPLY:

      3.   M81970-87-0012-C

      4.   870703

      5.   1005-00-921-5004

      6.   MAGAZINE ASSEMBLY, 30RD, 5.56MM

      7.A.   COOPER INDUSTRIES, UPLAND, CA 91786

      7.B.   30389

      7.C.   MCLB, ALBANY, GA 31704-5000

      8.   8448670

      9.   LOT 982/15A

      10.A.   DAAA09-81-C-4548

      10.B.   UNKNOWN

      10.C.   M819

      10.D.   UNK

M. A. BROWN, 808-1, 5291

                                          UNCLASSIFIED


ENCLOSURE (3)

UNCLASSIFIED

01   03                  PP         UUUU                      2301430

11.  NEW

12.  MAY 1983

13.  SEE NR 22

14.  NO

15.A.  500

15.B.  250

15.C.  250

15.D.  250

16.A.(1) M16A2, 5.56 MM RIFLE, NSN 1005-01-128-9936

16.A.(2) N/A

16.B.(1) N/A

16.B.(2) N/A

16.B.(3) N/A

16.B.(4) N/A

17.  $3.15

18.  $1,575.00

19.A.  UNKNOWN

19.B.  UNKNOWN

20.  N/A

21.  OTHER

M. A. BROWN, 808-1, 5291

UNCLASSIFIED

ENCLOSURE (3)

MCO 4855.10B
26 Jan 93

01   03            PP        UUUU                    2301430

22.   PROBLEM:  PER YOUR MSG 032118Z JUL 85, THIS BATTALION ORDERED

500 5.56MM 30RD MAGAZINES ON DOC NR M81970-7169-1528 TO REPLACE

THE COOPER MAGAZINES WE HELD.  THE REPLACEMENTS WE RECEIVED WERE

COOPER MAGAZINES AS WELL.  AFTER 5 MONTHS USE, THE NEW MAGAZINES

DEVELOPED SIMILAR PROBLEMS TO THOSE FOUND W/IN THE OLD MAGAZINES.

THEY EITHER FAILED TO FEED THE FINAL FIVE ROUNDS OR FAILED TO FEED

AT ALL.

     ACTION:  WE HAVE AGAIN RECALLED THE COOPER MAGAZINES HELD

W/IN THE BATTALION AND ARE REORDERING REPLACEMENTS.  WE WILL HOLD

THE DEFECTIVE ITEMS PENDING DISPOSITION INSTRUCTIONS.

     RECOMMENDATION:   IT IS RECOMMENDED THAT ALL COOPER

MAGAZINES BE REVIEWED FOR SERVICEABILITY AND POSSIBLE ELIMINATION.

23.   BLDG 3500, CAMP BROWN, CA 92055-5707.//

M. A. BROWN, 808-1, 5291

ENCLOSURE (3)

SAMPLE ELECTRONIC MAIL (E-MAIL) FOR THE CATEGORY I
PQDR

| QUALITY DEFICIENCY REPORT<br>Status: _____ | Category I or Category II<br>X |
|---|---|
| 1a. From (Originator)<br>NAME _____<br>STREET ADDRESS _____<br>CITY, STATE _____<br>DODAAC _____ | 2a. To (Screening Point)<br>NAME _____<br>STREET ADDRESS _____<br>CITY, STATE, ZIP _____<br>DODAAC _____ |
| 1b. Name, Phone & Signature<br>NAME _____<br>TITLE _____<br>AV/FTS   COMMERCIAL | 2b. Name, Phone & Signature<br>NAME _____<br>TITLE _____<br>AV/FTS   COMMERCIAL |
| 1c. Date (YYMMDD)<br>YYMMDD | 2c. Date (YYMMDD)<br>YYMMDD |

| 3. Report Control No.<br><br>12 A/N | 4. Date (YYMMDD)<br>Deficiency<br>Discovered<br>YYMMDD | 5. NSN<br><br><br>18 A/N |
|---|---|---|

| 6. Nomenclature<br><br>30 A/N | 7a. Manufacturer/City/State<br>MANUFACTURER _____<br>CITY, STATE |
|---|---|

| 7b. Mfrs. Code<br><br>8 A/N | 7c. Shipper/City/State<br>SHIPPER _____<br>CITY, STATE | 8. Mfrs. Part No.<br><br>20 A/N |
|---|---|---|

| 9. Ser/Lot/Batch No.<br>15 A/N<br>15 A/N<br>15 A/N (Up to 4<br>15 A/N Occurrences) | 10a. Contract No.<br>20 A/N<br><br>10b. Purchase Order No.<br>20 A/N | 10c. Requisition No.<br>20 A/N<br>20 A/N<br>20 A/N<br>20 A/N (Up to 4 Occurrences) |
|---|---|---|

| 10d. GBL No.<br><br><br>17 A/N | 11. Item<br><br><br>1 A/N | 12. Date (YYMMDD)<br>Recd, Mfrd,<br>Repaired or<br>Overhauled<br>6N | 13. Operating<br>Time at<br>Failure<br><br>7N | 14. Gov<br>Furn<br>Matl<br><br>1 A/N |
|---|---|---|---|---|

| 15. Quantity<br>UI ____ | a. Received<br>7 N | b. Inspected<br>7 N | c. Deficient<br>7 N | d. In Stock<br>7 N |
|---|---|---|---|---|

| 16. ___ Deficient<br>Item Works<br>On/With | a. End Item<br>(Aircraft,<br>Tank, etc.) | (1) Type/Model/Series<br><br>20 A/N | (2) Serial No.<br><br>15 A/N |
|---|---|---|---|

ENCLOSURE (4)

1

⟨25⟩

| 16b. Next Higher Assembly | (1) NSN 18 A/N | | (2) Nomenclature 20 A/N | |
|---|---|---|---|---|
| | (3) Part No. 20 A/N | | (4) Serial No. 20 A/N | |
| 17. Unit Cost 11 N | 18. Estimated Repair Cost 11 N | | 19a. Item Under Warranty 1 A/N | 19b. Expiration Date 6 N |
| 20. Work Unit Code/EIC (Navy and Air Force Only) 15 A/N | | 21. Action/Disposition 4 A/N (1 Character for code and 3 characters for days held) | | |

22. Details (            POC Name and Phone)

(A/N Variable Length--145 Lines Maximum)

23. Location of Deficient Material
9 A/N

| 24a. To (Action Point) NAME _____ ADDRESS _____ CITY, STATE, ZIP _____ DODAAC _____ | | 25A. To (Support Point) | | |
|---|---|---|---|---|
| 24b. Name, Phone, & Sign | 24c. Date | 25b. Name, Phone, & Sign | 25c. Date |
| 26a. To (Support Point) | | 27a. To (Support Point) | | |
| 26b. Name, Phone, & Sign | 26c. Date | 27b. Name, Phone, & Sign | 27c. Date |

ENCLOSURE (4)

2

(26)

| PRODUCT QUALITY DEFICIENCY REPORT | ☐ CATEGORY I | ☒ CATEGORY II |
|---|---|---|

| 1a. FROM (Originator) 2d Radio BN, 2d SRI Group, MMO Camp Lejeune, NC 28542 ACC: 21590 | | 2a. TO (Screening Point) Commander (Code 808-1) Marine Corps Logistics Bases Albany, GA 31704-5000 | | |
|---|---|---|---|---|
| 1b. NAME, TELEPHONE NO. AND SIGNATURE SSgt Griffith, S. E. 482-2990/1645 | 1c. DATE 25 Jul 91 | 2b. NAME, TELEPHONE NO. AND SIGNATURE Don DuBose, QA Specialist DSN 567-5291/92 | | 2c. DATE 23 Aug 91 |

| 3. REPORT CONTROL NO. M21590-91-03 | 4. DATE DEFICIENCY DISCOVERED 01 Jul 91 | 5. NATIONAL STOCK NO. (NSN) 5985-00-069-3744 | 6. NOMENCLATURE Antenna Element | 8. MFRS. PART NO. |
|---|---|---|---|---|
| 7a. MANUFACTURER/CITY/STATE Telex Comminucation, Inc. Nebraska | 7b. MFRS. CODE 15536 | 7c. SHIPPER/CITY/STATE Tobyhanna Lincoln Harrisburg, PA | | 870125 |
| 9. SERIAL/LOT/BATCH NO. N/A | 10a. CONTRACT NO. M67004-86-C-0058 | 10b. PURCHASE ORDER NO. N/A | 10c. REQUISITION NO. M21590-1155-7146 | 10d. GBL NO. N/A |

| 11. ITEM ☒ NEW ☐ REPAIRED/ OVERHAULED | 12. DATE RECD, MFRD, RE-PAIRED, OR OVERHAULED 01 Jul 91 | 13. OPERATING TIME AT FAILURE 0 Hrs | 14. GOVERNMENT FURNISHED MATERIAL ☐ YES ☒ NO |
|---|---|---|---|

| 15. QUANTITY | a. RECEIVED 1 | b. INSPECTED 1 | c. DEFICIENT 1 | d. IN STOCK 0 |
|---|---|---|---|---|

| 16. DEFICIENT ITEM WORKS ON/WITH | a. END ITEM (Aircraft, mower, etc.) | (1) TYPE/MODEL/SERIES AS-2851/TR Antenna 5985-00-097-8802 | | | (2) SERIAL NO. 2125 |
|---|---|---|---|---|---|
| | b. NEXT HIGHER ASSEMBLY | (1) NATIONAL STOCK NO. (NSN) 5985-00-069-3637 | (2) NOMENCLATURE Antenna Array Assy | (3) PART NO. 870361 | (4) SERIAL NO. N/A |

| 17. UNIT COST $ 22.23 | 18. ESTIMATED REPAIR COST $ 22.23 | 19a. ITEM UNDER WARRANTY ☐ YES ☐ NO ☒ UN-KNOWN | 19b. EXPIRATION DATE N/A |
|---|---|---|---|
| 20. WORK UNIT CODE/EIC (Navy and Air Force Only.) | | | |

| 21. ACTION/DISPOSITION ☒ HOLDING EXHIBIT FOR 60 DAYS ☐ RELEASED FOR INVESTIGATION ☐ RETURNED TO STOCK ☐ DISPOSED OF ☐ REPAIRED ☐ OTHER (Explain in Item 22) |
|---|

22. DETAILS (Describe, to best ability, what is wrong, how and why, circumstances prior to difficulty, description of difficulty, cause, action taken, including disposition, recommendations. Attach copies of supporting documents. Continue on separate sheet if necessary.)

NSN and P/N are correct when checked against MHIF (Dated 02/04/91) and IL (Dated 08/89 Fiche #03, Frame #C06, Item #02). However, item received is physically too long (Spec on IL is 4.854 ft., item is 5.75 ft. long).

| 23. LOCATION OF DEFICIENT MATERIAL 2d Radio BN, 2d SRI Group, (EM Section) Camp Lejeune, NC 28542 | | | | |
|---|---|---|---|---|
| 24a. TO (Action Point) DirTSD (Code 853) | | 25a. TO (Support Point) (Use Items 26 and 27 if more than one) | | |
| 24b. NAME, TELEPHONE NO. AND SIGNATURE | 24c. DATE | 25b. NAME, TELEPHONE NO. AND SIGNATURE | | 25c. DATE |
| 26a. TO (Support Point) | | 27a. TO (Support Point) | | |
| 26b. NAME, TELEPHONE NO. AND SIGNATURE | 26c. DATE | 27b. NAME, TELEPHONE NO. AND SIGNATURE | | 27c. DATE |

ENCLOSURE (5)

1

INSTRUCTIONS FOR PREPARATION OF THE PQDR (SF 368)

1. The originating point shall certify the PQDR for completeness, validity, and accuracy before it is submitted to the screening point. It is important to provide as much information as possible. Based on the nature of the deficiency and source of items, complete research may not be possible if all blocks are not completed. Block number 3 must be completed by the originating point before the report can be processed. The screening point will obtain correct or missing information from the originator, using telephone or electronic message, whenever possible.

    a. Instructions

        (1) Cat I/Cat II. See definitions.

        (2) Item 1a, FROM (Originator). Complete name of activity (no acronyms), Activity Address Code (AAC), and the address including ZIP Code of the addressee.

        (3) Item 1b, NAME, TELEPHONE NO. AND SIGNATURE. Provide name, telephone no. (include available telephone numbers; Federal Telephone System (FTS)_____, DSN, and commercial), and signature of an individual who can serve as a contact for questions regarding the report and/or request exhibits or samples.

        (4) Item 1c, DATE. Enter date report was signed and forwarded to the screening point.

        (5) Item 2a, TO (Screening Point). The originating point will complete the address with: Commander MARCORLOGBASES (Code 808-1), Albany, GA 31704-5000.

        (6) Item 2b, NAME, TELEPHONE NO. AND SIGNATURE. To be completed by the screening point.

        (7) Item 2c, DATE. The date the person finished processing the report at the screening point.

        (8) Item 3, REPORT CONTROL NO. Each report shall be identified by a control number consisting of the following: Unit RUC (six places), the calendar year for two places; and a sequential number starting with 0001 for each new year for four places, followed by the categorization of the PQDR (i.e., enter "C" for Cat I and "R" for Cat II) (e.g., M38010-89-0001R). If a contractor on site is originating the report, the first place

should be filled with an "O" followed by the applicable commercial and Government entity code, then the calendar year and sequential number (e.g., 053862-89-0001R). The DTG shall be shown in item 22 for the SF 368 follow-up on all Cat I PQDR's. The date in block 1c. for Cat I PQDR's submitted by E-Mail or electronic facsimile shall be shown in block 22 for the SF 368 follow-up.

(9) Item 4, DATE DEFICIENCY DISCOVERED. Enter the calendar date on which the deficiency was discovered.

(10) Item 5, NATIONAL STOCK NO. (NSN). Enter the NSN of the deficient materiel.

(11) Item 6, NOMENCLATURE. Enter the noun name of the materiel found to be deficient.

(12) Item 7a, MANUFACTURER/CITY/STATE. Enter name of the manufacturer (MFR), the maintenance contractor, or Government activity which last repaired or overhauled the deficient item. For motor vehicles or components thereof, enter name of MFR of the vehicle or component, as appropriate.

(13) Item 7b, MFRS CODE. Enter the name of the MFR and the Federal Supply five-digit code obtained from the Cataloging Handbook H4-1 and H4-2, the name of the shipper, or the name of the source of repair or overhaul.

(14) Item 7c, SHIPPER/CITY/STATE. When the shipper of an item is different from the MFR, also include the shipper or suppliers' name.

(15) Item 8, MFRS. PART NO. Enter the MFR's part number of the deficient item. Consult illustrated parts breakdown, technical manuals, supply publications, or similar sources to ensure correct identification of the items.

(16) Item 9, SERIAL/LOT/BATCH NO. As applicable, enter the serial number, lot number, or batch number of the deficient materiel. Use block 22 if additional space is required.

(17) Items 10a-10d, CONTRACT NO.: PURCHASE ORDER NO.; REQUISITION NO.: Government Bill of Lading (GBL) NO. Enter these numbers on any other available transportation document number in lieu of the Government Bill of Lading. Such numbers appear on the container, purchase document, and/or the item. It is extremely helpful if these items are furnished when the materiel was supplied by GSA.

ENCLOSURE (6)

(18) <u>Item 11, ITEM</u>.  Enter new or repaired/overhauled, as appropriate.  Refer to historical records, serviceable tags, etc., accompanying the items.

(19) <u>Item 12, DATE RECD.</u>, MFRD, REPAIRED, OR OVERHAULED.  Provide the dates manufactured and received, if available.

(20) <u>Item 13, OPERATING TIME AT FAILURE</u>.  Indicate the time the materiel has been in operation since new or overall/repair when the deficiency was discovered, using the appropriate performance element (i.e., miles, cycles, hours).  On a vehicle procured by GSA, also enter the calendar date on which the vehicle was placed in service.  Operating times for warranted equipment will be per the equipment SI or MFP.

(21) <u>Item 14, GOVERNMENT FURNISHED MATERIEL</u>.  Government Furnished Materiel is any materiel that belongs to the Government and is furnished to a contractor for production purposes.  Check the appropriate block as it applies.

(22) <u>Item 15, QUANTITY</u>

(a) <u>Item 15a, RECEIVED</u>.  Enter the total number of items received in a lot or batch in which the deficiency was found, if known.

(b) <u>Item 15b, INSPECTED</u>.  Enter the number of items in the lot or batch inspected.

(c) <u>Item 15c, DEFICIENT.</u>  Enter the number of items in the lot or batch which were determined to be deficient as a result of inspection.

(d) <u>Item 15d, IN STOCK</u>.  Enter the number of items in the lot or batch in stock at the facility reporting the deficiency. Provide a thorough explanation of this quantity in block 22.

(23) <u>Item 16, DEFICIENT ITEM WORKS ON/WITH</u>

(a) <u>Item 16a, END ITEM</u>.  List the major weapon system, item, or commodity the deficient item is to be used with or on (i.e., M16A2 Rifle, M198mm Howitzer, Hawk Guided Missile System). Indicate the NSN, type, model, series, and serial number for the end item, as applicable.

(b) <u>Item 16b, NEXT HIGHER ASSEMBLY</u>.  Enter the NSN, nomenclature, and part number of the next higher assembly the deficient item works on, as applicable.

(24) <u>Item 17, UNIT COST</u>.  Enter the dollar value of the deficient item when known.  N/A on reporting vehicles to GSA.

(25) Item 18, ESTIMATED REPAIR COST. Enter the unit cost times number of units for replacement or estimated repair costs (including overhead) times the number of units when it can readily be determined. Enter N/A on reporting vehicles to GSA.

(26) Item 19a, ITEM UNDER WARRANTY. Check the block to indicate whether the deficient item is covered by a contractual warranty, if known. (NOTE: SF 368 submitted under warranty must be per instructions included in the applicable MFP or 51.)

(27) Item 20, WORK UNIT CODE/EIC. Enter "N/A" as this block is N/A for Marine Corps.

(28) Item 21, ACTION/DISPOSITION. Check the appropriate block to indicate the action taken or requested. When an exhibit or sample is being held, indicate the number of days in the space provided. Maintain exhibits until the screening point calls for the materiel or for 60 days from receipt of the control number from the screening point. Reporting activities are reminded that the packing and shipping containers are to be held along with the exhibits to facilitate investigators. When none of the items indicate the actions or dispositions taken or requested, check "other" and identify the nature of the action taken or requested in block 22.

(29) Item 22, DETAILS. The following types of information should be entered:

(a) Explain what is wrong with the items. Include a description of the problem; the suspected cause if known; and identify action taken on the deficient materiel including disposition.

(b) Include recommendations, if readily available.

(c) Include and list the supporting documents to be submitted with the report. Photographs or sketches are extremely valuable and should be included whenever possible. (When photographs are taken, a 12-inch or other ruler should be employed as a scale placed alongside the object so as to appear in each photograph.) Measurements should also be shown on sketches.

(d) For tactical systems computer software, firmware, and documentation deficiencies, list the alphanumeric designator and/or title of other systems, computer programs, or documentation affected.

(e) When credit is desired, enter "Credit is requested under DoD 4000.25-7-M, Advice Code 024 applies." The requisition document number is required in all instances when credit is requested on the SF 368, even though a contract/purchase order is involved.

(f) Use additional paper and append to SF 368, as required.

(30) Item 23, LOCATION OF DEFICIENT MATERIAL. Enter the address and telephone number of the activity holding the exhibit if it is different from the PQDR originator address.

(31) Item 24a, TO (Action Point). The screening point shall enter in item 24a the name and address of the action point to which the report is being submitted. The action point, upon receipt, shall enter in items 24b-c the name, telephone number, signature, and date for the individual processing the report.

(32) Item 25a, TO (Support Point). The action point may fuse item 25a to identify the name and address of a support point to which the report is being submitted. The support point shall use item 25b to identify the name, telephone number, signature, and date for the individual it assigns to process the report. If more than one support point is involved, items 26 and 27 are used simultaneously.

(33) Item 26a, TO (Support Point). For use in addition to item 25, if needed.

(34) Item 27a, TO (Support Point). For use in addition to items 25 and 26, if needed.

(35) Item 28, FINDINGS AND RECOMMENDATIONS OF INVESTIGATION. Include the findings and recommendations for resolution of complaint.

(36) Item 29, ACTION TAKEN. State the action taken to resolve the complaint.

(37) Item 30, RESULTS OF DEPOT SURVEILLANCE. Show results of depot surveillance and planned action (i.e., replacement or repair by contractor, disposal, issue, etc.).

ENCLOSURE (6)

5

ORIGINATING POINT PROCEDURES

1.  The following tasks are required at the originating point, as applicable to the severity category of the PQDR:

   a.  For a Cat I PQDR

      (1) Suspend the use of deficient materiel to include any of the materiel in stock.  Maintain exhibits until the screening point calls for the materiel or for 60 days from receipt of the Marine Corps screening point number from the screening point.

      (2) Notify the Commander (Code 808-1), MARCORLOGBASES, Albany, Georgia, electronically by priority message or E-Mail using the SF 368 message or E-Mail format (enclosures (3) and (4)) or an electronic facsimile of the SF 368 (enclosure (5)).  Ensure the message contains Addressee Indicator Group 11216 on the information line to alert major Marine Corps commands and expedite the dissemination of supply/maintenance/logistics data on Cat I reports.  The message, E-Mail, or electronic facsimile of the SF 368 shall include the reasons for the suspension of use and other pertinent details.  The phone number for electronic facsimile is DSN 567-5631 or Commercial 912-439-5631.

      (3) Transmit Cat I PQDR's by oral communications, but confirm by message, E-Mail, or electronic facsimile when the urgency exists. The phone number for all oral communication is DSN 567-5291 or Commercial 912-439-5291.

      (4) Submit the SF 368 within 48 hours of the message, E-Mail, or electronic facsimile only when supporting documents will aid the investigation.  The SF 368 shall be prepared per enclosure (6).

   b.  For a Cat II PQDR

      (1) Suspend the use of the item or materiel as necessary.

      (2) Notify the Commander (Code 808-1), MARCORLOGBASES, Albany, Georgia, by E-Mail using the SF 368 format (enclosure (4)), electronic facsimile of the SF 368 or the SF 368 as outlined in enclosure (5).  The SF 368 will be submitted in triplicate, within 6 days after discovery of the deficiency, to Commander (Code 808-1), MARCORLOGBASES, Albany, GA 31704-5000.  Upon notification from the screening point that data/exhibits are not required, repair/overhaul and return the items to stock using the appropriate condition code or make disposition in the best interest of the Government.

c. _For all PQDR Categories_

(1) Maintain exhibits until the screening point calls for the materiel or for 60 days from receipt of the control number from the screening point.

(2) Submit exhibits for individual clothing on an "as required" basis as required by the screening point.

(3) Forward one information copy of each PQDR involving tactical digital systems computer software, firmware, and/or documentation deficiencies to the Commanding Officer, Marine Corps Tactical System Support Activity, Camp Pendleton, CA 92055-5130.

(4) The supporting maintenance activity will assist in the analysis and failure documentation prior to submission of the PQDR, when material deficiencies cannot be appropriately analyzed at a given user/maintenance level.

(5) Report any deficient PQDR responses to Commander (Code 808-1), MARCORLOGBASES, Albany, GA 31704-5000 (screening point), for corrective action.

(6) Maintain a status log on all PQDR's submitted through final action, noting final action taken, and maintain a copy of the finalized PQDR for a period of 1 year following final action per SECNAVINST P5212.5.

(7) Record the following entry on the SF 368 in block 22, when a PQDR is prepared and credit is desired for the deficient item, "Credit is requested under DoD 4000.25-7-M, Advice Code 024 applies only to PQDR reports." The requisition document number is required in all instances when credit is requested on the SF 368, even though a contract/purchase order is involved. When the original requisition number cannot be identified, the screening point will construct a 14 position Military Standard Requisitioning and Issue Procedures (MILSTRIP) document number for the PQDR.

(8) Obtain credit instructions through the Military Standard Billing System contained in DoD 4000.25-7-M.

(9) Report items known to be under warranty on the SF 368 per the implementing warranty clauses, SI's, or MFP's.

ENCLOSURE (7)

SCREENING POINT PROCEDURES

1. The Commander (Code 808-1), MARCORLOGBASES, Albany, Georgia, is designated as the screening point for Marine Corps PQDR's. The following are general procedures to be followed by the screening point:

    a. Assign screening point control numbers, to all PQDR's received from the originating points, using the last two digits of the calendar year and sequentially assigned control numbers (e.g., 840023). Enter in upper right-hand corner.

    b. Screen PQDR's per appendix A and validate category classification. In cases where the control number has been used previously, notify the originator and request a valid number.

    c. Ensure that the original MILSTRIP requisition document number is included on all SF 368's for defective materiel. When the original document number cannot be determined, the screening point will assign a MILSTRIP document number. The document number will be constructed as follows: the Department of Defense Activity Address Code (DODAAC) for the first six positions, the current Julian date (YDDD) for the next four positions, and a four-position serial number beginning with "U." An example of a constructed document number is M53121 8175 U001. In addition, when the original document number is not included, the screening point will include the DODAAC of the office to receive credit.

    d. Acknowledge receipt of each PQDR, and notify the originating point of the control number assigned in the following timeframe:

        (1) Cat I, within 24 hours by message.

        (2) Cat II, within 10 days.

    e. Provide instructions to the originating point and establish a new suspense date 30 calendar days from date data was requested, when the need for backup documentation, exhibits, photographs, etc., is obviously required. Process for investigation those deficiencies reported which may occasionally be received on the wrong form provided the format includes sufficient data for investigative purposes.

    f. Forward reports to the appropriate action point within the following timeframes:

        (1) Cat I, within 24 hours after receipt.

        (2) Cat II, within 10 days after receipt.

g. Forward a copy to the warranty administrator as identified by the appropriate SI or MFP, when the PQDR involves warranty provisions.

h. Complete PQDR's forwarded across DoD component lines per SECNAVINST 4855.5.

i. Provide disposition instructions for movement of all exhibits to originator when requested by action point. Make appropriate internal distribution of clothing samples as necessary for action.

j. Maintain historical files for each PQDR submitted per SECNAVINST P5212.5. Records should be retained for 1 year, provided corrective or other action has been completed.

k. Provide MARCORLOGBASES Depot Maintenance Activities (DMA) and Materiel Divisions with copies of all PQDR's and subsequent actions which have an affect on the DMA and Materiel Division's operations.

l. Monitor all reports on PQDR investigations through final action back to the originating point.

m. Perform follow-up actions and provide necessary data and interim and final status to originating points, services/agencies, commands, and contractors for appropriate action/information.

n. Maintain the design and operational portion of the MCQDIS.

o. Prepare the following quality analysis and provide the results to COMMARCORSYSCOM (PSE):

(1) Provide semiannually, the following PQDR's data analysis:

(a) Trend analyses of design/materiel deficiencies pertaining to contractors, commodities, originating services/agencies, etc.

(b) Average numbers/days to close Cat's I and II PQDR's.

(c) Comments on region and individual Contract Administration Office (CAO) data.

(2) Conduct semiannual evaluations of the overall adequacy and effectiveness of the system, including replies to deficiency reports, trend analysis, etc.

ENCLOSURE (8)

2

p.  Provide the standard monthly MCQDIS reports to the following addressees:

    (1) COMMARCORSYSCOM (PSE).

    (2) CG's.

       (a) FMFPac/FMFLant (G-4).

       (b) MCTSSA (ACM/QA).

       (c) Major Marine Corps commands when requested.

q.  Ensure that final responses to PQDR's are per DoDDir 4155.1 and SECNAVINST 4855.5 and adequately address the following:

    (1) Instructions to the originating point for exhibit disposition if not previously provided.

    (2) The PQDR report control number(s) and screening point control number on all replies and related correspondence.

    (3) The findings of any investigation conducted.

    (4) Action taken to correct the existing deficiencies.

    (5) Action taken to preclude recurrence.

    (6) Instructions for disposition of deficient materiel, when applicable.

    (7) The need for alert/field fix modification, if applicable.

    (8) Warranty provisions or latent defect clauses within the contract, if applicable.  This response should address two distinct areas:

       (a) Completion of warranty provisions that rectify the defect or failure and allows the equipment to be returned to full service use.

       (b) An analysis of the incident that provides data/ documentation sufficient to reveal design deficiencies or to track trends of incidents where the design is suspect.

    (9) Action taken to develop and release MI's, TI's, and SI's, as applicable.

    (10) Action taken to change stock listings and technical publications, if applicable.

r.  Prepare final/interim responses to the originator in the following timeframes:

(1) Cat I, within 3 days after receiving response from action point.

(2) Cat II, within 3 days after receiving response from action point.

s.  Ensure that integration/coordination is made with the Marine Corps Integrated Maintenance Management System.

t.  Ensure that all classified materiel received is controlled per OPNAVINST 5510.1.  Only blocks 3, 5, 6, and 16a(1) from the SF 368 will be loaded to the MCQDIS.  An entry of "classified" will be loaded to MCQDIS remarks field.

u.  Establish a training program to assure compliance with regulation and service implementing regulation in SECNAVINST 4855.5.

v.  Provide other screening points of known military users with results of the investigation and the corrective action, when appropriate.

# APPENDIX A

## SCREENING CRITERIA

| CONDITION | ACTION |
|---|---|
| • Inadequate information on form | Enter data from local/in-house sources or contact originator as soon as possible to obtain required information. |
| • Incorrect category classification | Upgrade or downgrade category classification as appropriate - provide justification explanation to originator. Category I classifications will not be used to expedite receipt of replacement part(s). |
| • Investigation already in progress from prior report | Provide action/support point with additional information including quantities requiring disposition instruction. |
| • Investigation on same problem just completed | Provide action/support point any additional information and request disposition instructions for additional quantity. |
| • Item damaged by user | Treat PQDR as invalid - terminate PQDR. |
| • No exhibit available | Check available stock for like deficiencies and/or check with originator to see if any additional data is available to confirm the defect. Recommend to action point that PQDR be classified as information only unless specific detailed narrative is available for use by the investigator. |
| • Deficiency encountered on materiel delivered on contracts closed over 4 years. | Process PQDR for possible investigation and screening of assets. |
| • Deficiency involves premature failure (other than new or newly overhauled product) | Treat PQDR as information only or, if considered to be a design problem, forward to action point for processing to appropriate support point for engineering investigation and corrective action. |
| • Noncontractor responsible deficiency | Process to action point with recommendation as to where investigation and corrective action should be directed. |
| • Involves warranted materiel | Treat all PQDRs on new warranted product as action. Treat all other PQDRs involving warranted materiel that failed during the warranty period, as information only and as a warranty claim. |
| • Improper storage | When storage problem was at a depot and not a field activity, forward to action point to request investigation by storage depot as to cause and corrective action. When storage damage is by user, terminate the PQDR. |
| • Item fails - normal wear and tear or after expected life. | Treat PQDR as invalid and terminate. |

Appendix A to
ENCLOSURE (8)

5

ACTION POINT PROCEDURES

1.  Timeframes for interim/final response to the screening point by severity category are as follows:

   a.  Cat I PQDR's.  Handle expeditiously and provide interim/ final response of actions within 20 days after receipt of investigation request without need for exhibit or 20 days after receipt of a requested exhibit.  If an extraordinary circumstance prevents the forwarding of a final reply during the mandatory 20-day reporting period, the action point shall furnish an interim reply to the screening point within that timeframe.  The action point shall subsequently furnish the screening point with an interim status report/reply on a monthly basis until the action point completes the investigation and forwards its final reply.

   b.  Cat II PQDR's.  Provide interim/final response within 30 days after receipt of investigation request without need for exhibit or 30 days after receipt of a requested exhibit.  If an extraordinary circumstance prevents the forwarding of a final reply during the mandatory 30-day reporting period, the action point shall furnish an interim reply to the screening point within that timeframe.  The action point shall subsequently furnish the screening point with an interim status report/reply on a monthly basis until the action point completes the investigation and forwards its final reply.

   c.  Acknowledgement.  Acknowledge receipt of each PQDR to the screening point within the following timeframes.

      (1) Cat I, within 24 hours.

      (2) Cat II, within 10 days.

2.  Provide the screening point (Commander (Code 808-1), MARCORLOGBASES, Albany, Georgia) with a copy of all reports and correspondence on PQDR actions taken.

3.  Request an exhibit/sample from the screening point on PQDR's as soon as the need for an exhibit/sample is known, but no later than 15 days from the date of receipt of PQDR when action point conducts independent investigation.

4.  Evaluate and coordinate PQDR's, prepare replies and take/initiate necessary corrective actions on PQDR's per this Order, and process each PQDR to meet suspense dates.

5.  Investigate the PQDR and take appropriate action to preclude recurrence of the deficiency.

6.  Take appropriate logistics management action when the PQDR indicates a need for such actions as: suspend procurements, stock screening, distribution of assets, or "warranty clause" actions.

7.  Initiate investigative actions by support points, as necessary, to finalize each report.  All action requests to the support point shall contain a statement of the specific support required and the pertinent background data which may be helpful in the investigation effort.  Prior to release of an action request, screen the PQDR to ensure all available or obtainable entries are complete and accurate and that the category assigned is correct.  Perform follow-up action and request status within 20 calendar days on a Cat I or 30 days on a Cat II after the date the report was sent by the action point to the support point if status is not furnished.

8.  Determine if the same identical deficiency is currently under investigation or has been resolved because of a previous report. If this situation does exist, a new investigation will not normally be initiated.  The current or previous investigation results may be used to reply to the screening point.  Forward a copy of the additional PQDR to the responsible support point for informational purposes and for ascertaining the contractor's position relative to repair/replacement of any additional defective materiel reported.

9.  Determine what closing action response the screening point should provide to the originating point, using the following criteria:

    a.  When the investigation of a PQDR determines that the reported conditions are not valid, the closing response to the originating point shall contain the reasons the report is considered invalid.

    b.  When the PQDR is found to be valid, the final reply shall:

    (1) Reference the subject report control number and screening point control number on all replies and related correspondence.

    (2) Provide the findings of the investigation conducted.

    (3) Provide the action taken to correct the existing deficiencies.

    (4) Provide the action taken to preclude recurrence.

    (5) Provide the disposition instructions for deficient stocks of materiel, when appropriate.

ENCLOSURE (9)

(6) Provide for alert notification, if applicable.

(7) Provide the existence of warranty provisions or latent defect clauses within the contract, if applicable.

(8) Provide the actions taken to change technical publications and stock lists, if applicable.

(9) Ensure integration with the Marine Corps Integrated Maintenance Management System.

(10) Provide a comment regarding recommendation for credit per DoD 4000.25-7-M. Provide the screening point (Commander (Code 808-1), MARCORLOGBASES, Albany, GA) the SF 368 responses for review and final closeout back to the originating point.

10. Complete the actions required on the reverse of each SF 368 (see enclosure (4)).

11. Develop as required, instructions for corrective action in the appropriate type of MI's and TI's, and submit such instructions for approval and release to the Commander (Code 850), MARCORLOGBASES, Albany, Georgia, for approval and release.

12. Provide a copy of the deficiency report to other affected participating components defined in MCO 8025.1.

13. Provide a copy of the final reply, with all pertinent documents, to the Defense Contract Management Command (DCMC), Quality Assurance Representative (QAR) for the QAR's contract file with one copy to the CAO for the official contract file, when applicable.

14. Evaluate the MCQDIS deficiency report data and the trend analysis provided by the screening point and direct management action toward resolution of recurring problems or adverse trends.

15. Establish liaison with integrated materiel managers and design agencies and forward requests for appropriate actions to these managers or agencies for resolution, as necessary, to the codes listed in SECNAVINST 4855.5.

16. Forward PQDR's received from the screening point resulting from materiel design or procurement deficiencies on interservice procurements to the cognizant activity which then becomes a support point. Coordinate planned Marine Corps actions required with the activity having specification, design, or technical responsibility. Channels of communication with each participating component are specified in SECNAVINST 4855.5.

17. Refer deficiency report cases to the CAO for necessary assistance or resolution when:

a.   It is established that the deficiency resulted from contractual requirements, including warranty provisions, which are. ambiguous, dubious, or otherwise questionable.

b.   The contractor refuses responsibility for or will not cooperate in evaluation of the deficiency, or where there is a possibility for repayment or recoupment of monies to or, from the contractor.

c.   There is a potential for the cause of the reported deficiency to have an impact on the quality of items currently in production under contract(s).

18.   Furnish information copies of PQDR's to the CAO when it is known that other contracts exist for the same item being reported as deficient, or when it is believed that the report may be of value in planning future actions.  Information copies of PQDR's will not require replies.

ENCLOSURE (9)

PQDR EXHIBIT PROCEDURES

1.  The following tasks are required to process PQDR exhibits:

    a.  Securing Exhibits.  All PQDR exhibits shall be secured/ segregated from all other materiel by the PQDR originating activity.  Exhibits shall be identified with a properly filled out DD Form 1575, Suspended Tag-Materiel, NSN 0102-LF-016-0400, and DD Form 2332, Product Quality Deficiency Report Exhibit, NSN 0102-LF-007-6400, and shall be classified in a suspended supply condition pending full implementation of supply Condition Code Q.

    b.  Exhibit Transportation Costs.  Unless otherwise provided for, transportation costs for shipping an exhibit to the investigation (e.g., contractor or other action point) will normally be the responsibility of the Government.  The contractor or action point is normally expected to bear transportation costs when exhibits are returned to the originating point or as otherwise requested.

    c.  Exhibit Shipping Priority Code.  The shipment of an exhibit(s) from an originator (holding) point to an action point for the conduct of an investigation shall be:

        (1) Cat I PQDR exhibits will be shipped Priority Designator (PD) 03(TP-1); Cat II PQDR exhibits will be shipped PD 06 (TP-2).

        (2) If specific shipping priority instructions are not provided for an exhibit to be returned after completion of an investigation, then the priority code PD 09(TP-3) shall be used.

    d.  Packaging and Marking.  Standard practice for commercial packaging may be used for exhibit packaging and marking guidance of exhibits.  The tagged exhibit (DD Form 1575 and DD Form 2332), along with a copy of the related deficiency report, shall be commercially packaged including necessary bracing and cushioning to ensure safe delivery to the destination.  The deficiency report shall identify the exhibit holding point, the name of a point of contact, and both commercial and Government (DSN, FTS, etc.) phone numbers.  The outside of the package shall be clearly marked "To Be Opened In The Presence Of A Government Representative" and shall also be marked "PQDR Exhibit/Report Control Number _____ and when applicable "Warranty Item."  MIL-STD-129 is applicable. For exhibits being returned to Canadian contractors, it is critical that the container be marked "U.S. Military Goods Returned For Investigation; Free Entry Under Tariff Item 70800-1, Materiel Deficiency Report Exhibits."  A copy of the shipping document shall be furnished the screening point on all exhibit movements.

e. <u>Exhibit Holding Time</u>.  Exhibits shall be held 60 days by the originating point or until disposition instructions are received from the screening point.  Exhibits shall not be repaired within the 60 day holding time unless critical mission requirements dictate.  In such circumstances, the originating point shall initiate appropriate action to retain evidence of the deficiency through photographs, testing, etc., that can be included with the PQDR.

f. <u>Action/Originating/Screening/Support Point Exhibit Responsibilities</u>.  Action/originating/screening/support point shall:

(1) Establish an information system to monitor the status of exhibit disposition instructions for compliance with requirements of figure 3.  The exhibit management system shall use the PQDR originator's report control number.

(2) Assure all disposition instructions relative to exhibits are accomplished using E-Mail or message processes.

g. <u>Exhibit Disposition (after completion of the investigation)</u>.  The screening point shall provide the action point with disposition instructions for exhibits.  In the event disposition instructions are not received by the action point by 30 days following a final investigation reply, a followup shall be conducted.  If disposition instructions are not received within 30 days after the followup, the action point shall prepare or request the contractor to prepare a DD Form 1149, Requisition, and Invoice/Shipping Document, identifying the Transportation Control Number related to the original shipment; and return the exhibit to the place from which it was received; and notify the action point of the shipment.  In the event the exhibit is obviously scrap materiel or the contractor fails to return the exhibit, the plant clearance officer will be requested by the DCMC Property Administrator to effect disposition and disposal under Federal Acquisition Regulation (FAR) 45.6.

h. Action points performing investigations shall provide management information, feedback data to the screening point identifying DODAAC's and report control numbers related to PQDR's for which exhibits have been requested and not received.

ENCLOSURE (10)

2

OUTPUT REQUIREMENTS FOR MARINE CORPS QUALITY
DEFICIENCY INFORMATION SYSTEM

1. The MCQDIS is an automated program managed by the screening point (Commander (Code 808-1), MARCORLOGBASES, Albany, Georgia) for tracking the status of PQDR's in process and maintaining a history of completed PQDR's. Four different formatted outputs are provided by the program as follows:

    a. <u>Report Number 1</u>. Consists of PQDR status by reporting unit in reporting control number sequence. This report serves as the base history for every PQDR submitted by any Marine Corps activity.

    b. <u>Report Number 2</u>. Consists of PQDR status by the defective item NSN. This report depicts trends of the defective items as they pertain to an end item or to a multitude of end items. This report includes additional data elements now available in the base file. PQDR's received after April 1987 contain the additional data.

    c. <u>Report Number 3</u>. Consists of PQDR status by major end item NSN. This report depicts trends of the major end item as it relates to the defective items, geographical locations, and contract number.

    d. <u>Report Number 4</u>. Consists of PQDR status by action points. This report shows the action taken, as well as depicting positive responses, negative responses, or the lack of responses.

ENCLOSURE (1)

1

www.ingramcontent.com/pod-product-compliance
Lightning Source LLC
Chambersburg PA
CBHW080616290526
45790CB00007B/2799